A Comprehensive Handbook for Budgerigars (Budgies/Parakeets)

Your Complete Guide to Budgerigars Care, Companionship, and Connection

Maxwell Aviary

Table of Contents

INTRODUCTION   6

1 | OVERVIEW OF BUDGERIGARS   8

History and Origin   10

Physical Characteristics   12

2 | CHOOSING YOUR BUDGERIGAR   16

Finding a Reputable Breeder or Rescue   16

Selecting a Healthy Budgerigar   19

Considerations for Color Varieties   22

3 | PREPARING FOR YOUR BUDGERIGAR   26

Setting Up the Perfect Environment   26

Cage Selection and Placement   29

Necessary Accessories and Supplies   32

4 | BUDGERIGAR DIET AND NUTRITION   36

Understanding Budgerigar's Nutritional Needs   36

Fresh Foods vs. Commercial Diets   39

Safe and Unsafe Foods for Budgerigars   42

Water Requirements   45

5 | BUDGERIGAR HEALTH AND WELLNESS   48

Signs of a Healthy Budgerigar   48

Common Health Issues and Diseases   51

Regular Veterinary Check-ups   54

First Aid and Emergency Care   56

6 | BEHAVIORAL ASPECTS OF BUDGERIGARS   62

Bonding with Your Budgerigar   62

Understanding Budgerigar Communication   65

Training and Socialization Techniques   67

Dealing with Behavioral Problems in Budgerigars   71

7 | ENRICHMENT AND ENTERTAINMENT   76

Providing Mental Stimulation   76

Toys and Activities for Budgerigars   79

Safe Out-of-Cage Time   82

8 | BREEDING AND REPRODUCTION   86

Breeding Considerations   86

Nesting and Egg Incubation   89

Caring for Budgerigar Chicks   93

9 | LONGEVITY AND END-OF-LIFE CARE   97

Budgerigar Lifespan   97

Quality of Life Considerations   99

Palliative Care and Euthanasia   102

10 | BUDGERIGAR ETIQUETTE AND LEGAL
CONSIDERATIONS   105

Responsible Ownership Practices   105

Legal Requirements and Regulations   107

Interactions with Other Pets   110

CONCLUSION   114

INTRODUCTION

Welcome to the fascinating world of Budgerigars, affectionately known as Budgies or Parakeets! Whether you're a seasoned bird enthusiast or embarking on your first avian adventure, you're in for a delightful journey with these charming and intelligent creatures.

Imagine waking up to the melodious chirps of your Budgie, a cheerful greeting that brightens even the dreariest of mornings. Picture their vibrant plumage, ranging from electric blues to sunny yellows, adorning your living space with a splash of color and vitality. But beyond their beauty lies a bond unlike any other, as Budgerigars possess a unique ability to capture our hearts with their endearing quirks and playful antics.

In this comprehensive guide, we'll delve into every aspect of caring for Budgerigars as beloved companions. From understanding their origins and distinctive traits to creating the perfect habitat and fostering a deep connection, each chapter is crafted to empower you as a responsible and compassionate pet owner.

Join me as we unravel the secrets of Budgerigar care, nurturing not just feathered friends, but cherished members of the family. Whether you're seeking guidance on nutrition, health, behavior, or simply looking to deepen your understanding of these captivating creatures, this book is your roadmap to building a fulfilling and enriching relationship with your Budgie.

So, embark on this enchanting journey with an open heart and a curious mind, for the world of Budgerigars awaits with boundless joy and wonder. Let's spread our wings and soar into a world where every chirp, every flutter, is a testament to the beauty of companionship between humans and birds.

1 | OVERVIEW OF BUDGERIGARS

Budgerigars, affectionately known as Budgies, are small parrots native to Australia, particularly found in the arid regions of the continent. These delightful birds have been cherished as pets for decades, admired for their striking appearance, charming personality, and remarkable intelligence.

In their natural habitat, Budgerigars are highly adaptable, thriving in a variety of environments ranging from open grasslands to dense scrublands. They are known for their nomadic lifestyle, forming large flocks that roam in search of food and water. This social behavior is ingrained in their nature and reflects their need for companionship and interaction.

Size-wise, Budgerigars are petite, typically measuring around 7 inches (18 centimeters) in length from beak to tail. Their wingspan spans approximately 10 inches (25 centimeters), allowing for agile flight and graceful movement. What truly sets Budgies apart, however, is their stunning plumage. Their feathers come in an array of colors, including vibrant blues, greens, yellows, and whites, often adorned with intricate patterns and markings unique to each individual.

Beyond their physical beauty, Budgerigars are renowned for their sociable and inquisitive personalities. They are naturally curious creatures, eager to explore their surroundings and engage in playful activities. Budgies thrive on interaction, forming strong bonds not only with their human caregivers but also with other Budgies in their flock or household. This social aspect of their nature makes them excellent companions for individuals and families alike.

Communication is another fascinating aspect of Budgerigar behavior. These birds are highly vocal, using a variety of chirps, whistles, and squawks to express themselves and communicate with others. With patience and training, Budgies can even learn to mimic human speech, adding an extra layer of charm to their already endearing personalities.

In terms of diet, Budgerigars are primarily seed-eaters in the wild, consuming a variety of grass seeds, grains, and vegetation. However, as pets, they require a balanced diet that goes beyond just seeds. A high-quality commercial seed mix forms the foundation of their diet, supplemented with fresh fruits, vegetables, and occasional treats to ensure they receive essential nutrients and vitamins for optimal health and well-being.

Overall, Budgerigars are beloved companions known for their intelligence, sociability, and beauty. Whether perched on your shoulder, entertaining you with their antics, or serenading you with their sweet chirps, Budgies have a special way of brightening your day and warming your heart. With proper care, attention, and affection, these captivating birds flourish in captivity, enriching the lives of their human companions in countless ways.

History and Origin

The history of Budgerigars is as rich and colorful as their plumage. These charming birds have been intertwined with human culture for centuries, captivating the hearts of people around the world with their beauty and personality.

Budgerigars, scientifically known as Melopsittacus undulatus, are native to Australia, where they have existed for thousands of years. The Aboriginal people of Australia were likely the first to encounter Budgerigars in their natural habitat, observing their graceful flight and melodic calls in the wild. These birds were not only admired for their striking appearance but also respected for their role in the ecosystem as seed dispersers and pollinators.

The first recorded European encounter with Budgerigars occurred in the late 18th century when Dutch explorer and navigator, Captain Willem de Vlamingh, landed on the western coast of Australia in 1697. He described seeing colorful parakeets flying in flocks and noted their resemblance to the European Parakeet (now known as the Alexandrine Parakeet). However, it wasn't until the early 19th century that Budgerigars began to attract widespread attention from European naturalists and collectors.

In 1805, English naturalist John Gould formally described the Budgerigar in his book "Birds of Europe." He gave them the scientific name "Melopsittacus undulatus," derived from Greek words meaning "melodious" and "undulating," in reference to their musical calls and wavy plumage markings.

Budgerigars quickly gained popularity among European bird enthusiasts, thanks to their striking appearance and engaging personalities. They were first imported to England in the mid-19th century, where they became prized specimens in aviaries and private collections. The demand for Budgerigars soon spread to other parts of Europe and eventually to North America and beyond.

The commercial breeding of Budgerigars for the pet trade began in earnest in the early 20th century, with breeders selectively breeding for desirable traits such as color mutations and tameness. These efforts resulted in the wide variety of Budgerigar color mutations seen in captivity today, ranging from the classic green and yellow to more exotic shades of blue, violet, and albino.

Today, Budgerigars are one of the most popular pet birds worldwide, cherished for their beauty, intelligence, and sociable nature. They have also become subjects of scientific research, with studies exploring their vocal learning abilities, cognitive skills, and behavior.

Despite their widespread popularity as pets, Budgerigars still inhabit their native Australian habitats, where they continue to thrive in the wild. However, habitat loss, introduced predators, and other human-induced pressures pose significant challenges to their survival in their native range, highlighting the importance of conservation efforts to protect these iconic birds for future generations to enjoy.

Physical Characteristics

Budgerigars, also known as Budgies or Parakeets, possess a distinctive combination of physical features that make them instantly recognizable and utterly charming. From their petite size to their vibrant plumage, Budgerigars captivate the hearts of bird enthusiasts worldwide.

1. **Size and Shape**: Budgerigars are small parrots, typically measuring around 7 inches (18 centimeters) in length from beak to tail. They have a compact, streamlined body with a short, rounded tail and a slightly curved beak. Their wings are proportionate to their body size, allowing for agile flight and nimble maneuvers.

2. **Plumage**: One of the most striking features of Budgerigars is their colorful plumage. In the wild, the typical Budgie sports a bright green body with yellow markings on the head and wings, black markings on the nape, and black barring on the wings and back. However, selective breeding has produced a wide array of color mutations, including blue, violet, white, and various combinations thereof. These color variations add to the allure of Budgerigars as pets, offering endless possibilities for unique and eye-catching companions.

3. **Head and Beak**: Budgerigars have small, rounded heads with expressive, dark eyes that convey curiosity and intelligence. Their beaks are short and conical,

designed for cracking open seeds and manipulating small objects. The upper mandible slightly overlaps the lower mandible, allowing for precise control and dexterity when feeding and exploring.

4. **Feet and Legs**: Budgerigars have sturdy feet with four toes, two pointing forward and two pointing backward. This arrangement, known as zygodactyl feet, provides them with a strong grip for perching and climbing. Their legs are relatively short but well-suited for hopping and maneuvering within their environment.

5. **Sexual Dimorphism**: Male and female Budgerigars exhibit subtle differences in physical appearance, particularly in the cere—the fleshy area above the beak where the nostrils are located. In adult males, the cere typically appears blue or purplish-blue, while in adult females, it tends to be beige, brown, or pale blue. Additionally, some color mutations may affect the appearance of the cere, making it a less reliable indicator of sex in certain cases.

Overall, the physical characteristics of Budgerigars reflect their adaptation to a life of agility, social interaction, and exploration. Whether observed in the wild or admired as pets, Budgies embody a unique blend of beauty, grace, and charm that continues to enchant bird lovers of all ages.

2 | CHOOSING YOUR BUDGERIGAR

Finding a Reputable Breeder or Rescue

Choosing where to acquire your Budgerigar is a significant decision that impacts not only your experience as a pet owner but also the welfare of the bird you bring into your home. Whether you opt for a breeder or a rescue organization, ensuring that you're obtaining your Budgie from a reputable source is paramount.

Finding a Reputable Breeder:

1. **Research and Reputation**: Start by researching breeders in your area or online. Look for breeders with positive reviews and a strong reputation within the avian community. Seek recommendations from fellow bird enthusiasts or consult online forums and social media groups dedicated to bird keeping.

2. **Transparency and Communication**: A reputable breeder will be transparent about their breeding practices and the health of their birds. They should be willing to answer your questions and provide documentation, such as health certificates and genetic

testing results. Communication is key, so don't hesitate to reach out and ask for information.

3. **Visit the Breeder**: Whenever possible, visit the breeder's facility in person to assess the conditions in which the birds are raised. Pay attention to cleanliness, space, and the overall health and well-being of the birds. A reputable breeder will maintain a clean and healthy environment for their birds and provide appropriate socialization and enrichment.

4. **Health Guarantees and Support**: Choose a breeder who offers health guarantees for their birds and provides ongoing support and advice to new owners. A responsible breeder will be committed to the welfare of their birds and will be available to assist you with any questions or concerns that may arise after bringing your Budgie home.

Adopting from a Rescue Organization:

1. **Research Rescue Organizations**: Look for reputable rescue organizations or avian sanctuaries that specialize in caring for and rehoming Budgerigars. These organizations often have birds available for adoption and can provide valuable

information about their backgrounds and temperaments.

2. **Assessing Compatibility**: When considering adoption, take the time to interact with the Budgies available for adoption and assess their compatibility with your lifestyle and preferences. Rescue organizations may conduct behavioral assessments to match birds with suitable adopters.

3. **Understanding Rehabilitation Needs**: Some rescued Budgerigars may have special needs or require rehabilitation due to previous neglect or trauma. Be prepared to provide patience, understanding, and a supportive environment as your new feathered friend adjusts to their new home.

4. **Adoption Process and Requirements**: Follow the adoption process outlined by the rescue organization, which may include filling out an application, undergoing a home visit, and paying an adoption fee. These requirements are in place to ensure that the birds are placed in loving and responsible homes.

Regardless of whether you choose to purchase from a breeder or adopt from a rescue organization, the most important consideration is the well-being of the Budgerigar.

Selecting a Healthy Budgerigar

Choosing a healthy Budgerigar is crucial for ensuring a long and happy life for your feathered friend. Whether you're purchasing from a breeder or adopting from a rescue organization, there are several key factors to consider when selecting your Budgie.

1. **Physical Appearance**:

   - **Feathers**: Look for a Budgerigar with smooth, sleek feathers that lie flat against the body. Avoid birds with ruffled or fluffed feathers, as this could indicate illness or poor health.

   - **Eyes**: The eyes should be bright, clear, and free from any discharge or crustiness. Cloudy or dull eyes may be a sign of illness or underlying health issues.

   - **Nostrils**: Check the nostrils for any signs of discharge, blockages, or swelling. Healthy

Budgies have clean, dry nostrils without any visible abnormalities.

- **Beak and Feet**: The beak should be smooth, symmetrical, and free from any deformities or overgrowth. Similarly, the feet should be clean, dry, and free from any swelling or abnormalities.

2. **Behavior**:

- **Alertness**: A healthy Budgerigar is alert, active, and curious about its surroundings. Look for birds that are responsive to stimuli and show interest in interacting with you.

- **Vocalization**: Pay attention to the Budgie's vocalizations. Healthy Budgies chirp and vocalize regularly, expressing curiosity and contentment. Be cautious of birds that are unusually quiet or exhibit wheezing or raspy sounds when breathing.

- **Movement**: Watch the Budgie's movements to assess its agility and coordination. Healthy birds move with ease, hopping around their enclosure and perching confidently. Avoid birds that appear lethargic, unsteady, or have difficulty moving.

3. **Socialization**:

   - **Interaction**: Spend time observing how the Budgerigars interact with each other and with humans. Look for birds that are comfortable with human presence and show interest in interacting with you.

   - **Compatibility**: Consider the Budgie's compatibility with other birds if you plan to keep multiple Budgies. Choose birds that get along well and exhibit positive social behaviors, such as preening each other or sharing food and toys.

4. **Health History and Documentation**:

   - **Health Records**: Request health records and documentation from the breeder or rescue organization, including vaccination records, genetic testing results, and any history of medical treatments or illnesses.

   - **Veterinary Check-up**: Schedule a veterinary check-up for your Budgie shortly after acquiring it, regardless of its apparent health status. A qualified avian veterinarian can perform a thorough examination and provide recommendations for care and preventive measures.

5. **Trust Your Instincts**:

- Trust your instincts and intuition when selecting a Budgerigar. If something feels off or if you have doubts about the bird's health or background, it's best to err on the side of caution and explore other options.

Considerations for Color Varieties

Budgerigars come in a dazzling array of colors and patterns, thanks to selective breeding efforts that have produced a wide range of color mutations. When selecting a Budgerigar, considering the various color varieties available can add an extra layer of excitement and personalization to your choice. Here are some key considerations for exploring the world of Budgerigar color varieties:

1. **Classic Green and Yellow**:

- The classic green and yellow Budgerigars are the most commonly seen color combination in the wild and among pet Budgies.

- Green Budgies typically have a bright green body with yellow markings on the head, wings, and abdomen, while yellow Budgies display a predominantly yellow plumage with green accents.

2. **Blue Varieties**:

- Blue Budgerigars are characterized by a predominantly blue plumage, ranging from sky blue to deep cobalt blue.

- Some blue Budgies may have white or lighter blue markings on the head, wings, or tail, adding variation and interest to their appearance.

3. **White Varieties**:

- White Budgerigars, also known as albino or lutino Budgies, have a predominantly white plumage with little to no color pigment.

- Albino Budgies have red eyes and lack melanin pigment, resulting in a pure white appearance, while lutino Budgies have pink or red eyes and exhibit yellow or pale orange feathering.

4. **Grey and Violet Varieties**:

   - Grey Budgerigars, also known as greywings or clearwings, have a dilute grey or silver plumage with lighter markings compared to their wild-type counterparts.

   - Violet Budgerigars exhibit a purple or violet hue to their plumage, adding a touch of richness and depth to their coloration.

5. **Spangle and Opaline Varieties**:

   - Spangle Budgerigars have bold, contrasting markings on their feathers, giving them a striking and eye-catching appearance.

   - Opaline Budgies have a unique feather pattern that creates a lacy or marbled effect, adding a sense of elegance and sophistication to their appearance.

6. **Combination Varieties**:

- Many Budgerigars exhibit combinations of different color mutations, resulting in a kaleidoscope of hues and patterns.

- For example, you may find Budgies with combinations of blue and white, yellow and green, or grey and violet, each with its own unique charm and personality.

When selecting a Budgerigar based on color variety, it's essential to consider your personal preferences, as well as the availability and genetic diversity of the birds. Keep in mind that while color mutations add visual interest and diversity to the Budgie population, it's crucial to prioritize the overall health, temperament, and well-being of the bird above all else. Whether you prefer the classic green and yellow Budgie or a more exotic and colorful variety, each Budgerigar brings its own unique beauty and charm to your home.

3 | PREPARING FOR YOUR BUDGERIGAR

Setting Up the Perfect Environment

Creating an ideal environment for your Budgerigar is essential for their physical health, mental well-being, and overall happiness. Whether you're welcoming a new Budgie into your home or upgrading their living space, thoughtful consideration and attention to detail are key to setting up a perfect environment. Here's how to do it:

1. **Choosing the Right Cage**:

    - Selecting an appropriate cage is the foundation of creating a perfect environment for your Budgerigar. Choose a cage that is spacious enough to allow for ample movement, stretching, and flying within the confines of their home.

    - The cage should be made of safe, non-toxic materials, with bars spaced closely enough to prevent escape or injury. Opt for horizontal bars to facilitate climbing and perching.

- Consider the placement of doors and access points for ease of cleaning and maintenance. Additionally, choose a cage with a secure locking mechanism to prevent accidental openings.

2. **Location, Location, Location**:

- Where you place the cage within your home can greatly impact your Budgie's well-being. Select a location that provides a balance of natural light and shade, away from direct sunlight and drafts.

- Position the cage at eye level or slightly above to encourage interaction and engagement with your Budgie. Avoid placing the cage in isolated or high-traffic areas, as this can cause stress or discomfort for your feathered friend.

3. **Creating a Comfortable Interior**:

- Once you have the cage in place, focus on making the interior a cozy and inviting space for your Budgie. Line the bottom of the cage with a suitable substrate, such as paper or cage liners, to absorb droppings and provide a comfortable surface for walking.

- Add a variety of perches, branches, and platforms of different sizes and textures to encourage natural behaviors like climbing and perching. Avoid using sandpaper perches, as they can cause abrasions on your Budgie's feet.

- Introduce a selection of toys and enrichment activities to keep your Budgie mentally stimulated and entertained. Include items like bells, mirrors, swings, and puzzle toys to encourage exploration and play.

4. **Nutrition and Hydration Stations**:

- Ensure that food and water dishes are easily accessible and securely attached to the cage. Choose dishes that are easy to clean and made of non-toxic materials.

- Provide a balanced diet consisting of high-quality commercial seed mixes supplemented with fresh fruits, vegetables, and occasional treats. Ensure that food is replaced regularly to maintain freshness and prevent contamination.

- Offer clean, fresh water daily in a separate dish or water dispenser. Regularly clean and refill water dishes to prevent bacterial growth and ensure hydration for your Budgie.

5. **Maintaining Cleanliness and Hygiene**:

   - Establish a regular cleaning routine to keep the cage and surrounding area clean and hygienic. Remove droppings, leftover food, and soiled substrate daily, and conduct a thorough cleaning of the cage on a weekly basis.

   - Wash food and water dishes regularly with mild soap and warm water to prevent bacterial buildup and contamination. Allow dishes to air dry completely before refilling.

   - Monitor your Budgie's health and behavior closely, and seek veterinary attention if you notice any signs of illness or distress.

Cage Selection and Placement

Choosing the right cage and strategically placing it within your home are crucial steps in creating a safe, comfortable, and stimulating environment for your Budgerigar. Here's a detailed guide to help you make informed decisions:

Cage Selection:

1. **Size Matters**: Opt for the largest cage your space and budget allow. Budgerigars are active birds that require room to move, stretch their wings, and explore. A spacious cage provides them with the physical and mental stimulation they need for a happy and healthy life.

2. **Bar Spacing**: Choose a cage with horizontal bars spaced no more than 1/2 inch apart. This prevents your Budgie from getting stuck or injured and allows for easy climbing and perching.

3. **Materials**: Select a cage made of safe, non-toxic materials. Stainless steel and powder-coated metal cages are durable and easy to clean. Avoid cages made of zinc or lead, as they can be toxic to birds if ingested.

4. **Accessibility**: Look for a cage with multiple doors for easy access to your Budgie and their belongings. Removable trays and grates facilitate cleaning, while secure latches prevent accidental escapes.

5. **Additional Features**: Consider cages with built-in features such as seed guards to contain mess, playtops for extra space and enrichment, and rolling casters for easy mobility.

Cage Placement:

1. **Light and Airflow**: Place the cage in a well-lit area with natural light, but avoid direct sunlight, which can overheat your Budgie. Ensure adequate airflow and ventilation to maintain a comfortable temperature and prevent stagnant air.

2. **Temperature Regulation**: Avoid placing the cage near drafts, air vents, or heating/cooling sources, as sudden temperature fluctuations can stress your Budgie. Aim for a stable temperature range of 65-80°F (18-27°C).

3. **Quiet and Calm**: Position the cage away from noisy appliances, televisions, and high-traffic areas to minimize stress and disturbance for your Budgie. Provide a quiet and calm environment where they can relax and feel secure.

4. **Social Interaction**: Place the cage at eye level or slightly above to encourage social interaction and bonding between you and your Budgie. Avoid isolating them in low or secluded areas, as this can lead to loneliness and boredom.

5. **Security and Comfort**: Ensure that the cage is securely anchored and stable to prevent tipping or

falling. Place the cage against a wall or in a corner to provide a sense of security and enclosure for your Budgie.

By carefully selecting a suitable cage and thoughtfully placing it within your home, you can create a safe, comfortable, and enriching environment where your Budgie can thrive and flourish. Regularly assess their living space and make adjustments as needed to meet their evolving needs and preferences.

Necessary Accessories and Supplies

Equipping your Budgerigar's living space with essential accessories and supplies is vital for ensuring their comfort, health, and overall well-being. From perches to toys to grooming tools, here's a comprehensive list of items you'll need to create a safe and stimulating environment for your feathered friend:

1. **Perches**: Provide a variety of perches of different sizes, shapes, and textures to promote foot health and prevent boredom. Natural wood perches, rope perches, and cement perches are excellent options that offer variety and stimulation.

2. **Toys**: Stimulate your Budgie's mind and body with a selection of toys designed for birds. Include toys such as swings, bells, mirrors, shreddable toys, and puzzle toys to encourage play, exploration, and mental stimulation.

3. **Food and Water Dishes**: Choose durable, easy-to-clean dishes made of ceramic or stainless steel for serving food and water. Ensure that dishes are securely attached to the cage to prevent tipping and contamination.

4. **Cage Liners or Substrate**: Line the bottom of the cage with cage liners, paper, or substrate to absorb droppings and provide a clean and comfortable surface for your Budgie. Avoid using sandpaper or walnut shell substrates, as they can be abrasive and harmful to your Budgie's feet.

5. **Cuttlebone and Mineral Blocks**: Offer cuttlebone or mineral blocks to provide essential calcium and minerals for your Budgie's bone health and beak maintenance. These items also offer a natural outlet for chewing and foraging behavior.

6. **Grooming Supplies**: Keep your Budgie looking and feeling their best with grooming supplies such as nail

clippers, beak trimmers, and a bird-safe grooming perch or platform. Regular grooming helps prevent overgrown nails and beak, promoting optimal health and comfort.

7. **Bath Tub or Spray Bottle**: Allow your Budgie to indulge in their natural bathing instincts by providing a shallow dish of water for bathing or using a spray bottle to mist them gently. Regular baths help keep their feathers clean and healthy.

8. **First Aid Kit**: Keep a bird-specific first aid kit on hand for treating minor injuries or emergencies. Include items such as styptic powder, antibiotic ointment, gauze pads, and a pet-safe antiseptic solution.

9. **Health and Identification**: Invest in a leg band or microchip for permanent identification in case your Budgie gets lost. Additionally, schedule regular check-ups with an avian veterinarian to monitor their health and address any concerns.

10. **Travel Carrier**: Have a sturdy, well-ventilated travel carrier on hand for transporting your Budgie safely and comfortably when necessary, such as visits to the veterinarian or travel.

11. **Educational Resources**: Equip yourself with books, online resources, and information about Budgerigar care, behavior, and health to ensure you're well-prepared to meet your Budgie's needs and provide the best possible care.

By stocking up on these necessary accessories and supplies, you'll be well-equipped to create a nurturing and enriching environment for your Budgerigar, fostering their physical and mental well-being and strengthening the bond between you and your feathered companion.

4 | BUDGERIGAR DIET AND NUTRITION

Understanding Budgerigar's Nutritional Needs

Proper nutrition is fundamental to the health and well-being of your Budgerigar. Understanding their nutritional needs is crucial for providing a balanced diet that supports their growth, development, and overall vitality. Budgerigars have specific dietary requirements influenced by factors such as age, activity level, and health status. Let's delve into the key components of their nutritional needs:

1. **Seeds and Pellets**:

    - Seeds have been a traditional staple in a Budgerigar's diet, providing essential nutrients such as carbohydrates, fats, and protein. However, seeds alone are not sufficient to meet all of their dietary requirements.

    - Commercially formulated pellets offer a more balanced and complete diet, providing essential vitamins, minerals, and other nutrients in a convenient and uniform manner. Pellets also help prevent selective feeding, where Budgies pick out their favorite seeds and neglect other essential nutrients.

2. **Fresh Fruits and Vegetables**:

- Fresh fruits and vegetables are essential components of a Budgerigar's diet, providing essential vitamins, minerals, fiber, and antioxidants. Offer a variety of fruits and vegetables such as apples, carrots, broccoli, spinach, and bell peppers.

- Introduce new fruits and vegetables gradually to allow your Budgie to adjust to different flavors and textures. Wash fruits and vegetables thoroughly to remove any pesticides or contaminants before serving.

3. **Protein Sources**:

- Budgerigars require adequate protein for muscle development, feather health, and overall growth. Offer protein-rich foods such as cooked eggs, legumes (e.g., lentils, chickpeas), and small amounts of lean cooked meat (e.g., chicken or turkey) as occasional treats.

- Avoid feeding your Budgie high-fat or high-sodium protein sources, such as fatty meats or processed meats, as these can lead to health issues such as obesity and heart disease.

4. **Calcium and Mineral Supplements**:

- Calcium is essential for Budgerigars to maintain strong bones, eggshell formation (for breeding females), and overall health. Offer calcium-rich foods such as cuttlebone, mineral blocks, and dark leafy greens.

- Provide access to a mineral supplement specifically formulated for birds to ensure they receive essential trace minerals and micronutrients.

5. **Hydration**:

- Fresh, clean water should be available to your Budgerigar at all times. Change the water daily to prevent bacterial growth and contamination. Consider using a water dispenser or bottle to prevent spillage and keep the water clean.

6. **Avoiding Toxic Foods**:

- Certain foods are toxic to Budgerigars and should be avoided at all costs. These include avocado, chocolate, caffeine, alcohol, and foods high in salt, sugar, or fat. These substances can cause serious health issues and even be fatal to Budgies if ingested

Fresh Foods vs. Commercial Diets

When it comes to providing nutrition for your Budgerigar, you'll encounter two primary options: fresh foods and commercial diets (seeds and pellets). Each option has its advantages and considerations, and understanding the differences between them can help you make informed decisions about your Budgie's diet.

Fresh Foods:

1. **Nutrient Variety**: Fresh foods, including fruits, vegetables, and protein sources like eggs and cooked meat, offer a wide range of essential nutrients, vitamins, and minerals. These nutrients support overall health, immune function, and vitality in Budgerigars.

2. **Palatability and Variety**: Fresh foods provide variety in taste, texture, and presentation, making mealtimes more interesting and enjoyable for your Budgie. Offering a diverse selection of fresh foods encourages natural foraging behaviors and stimulates their curiosity.

3. **Hydration**: Many fresh fruits and vegetables have high water content, contributing to your Budgie's hydration needs. This is particularly beneficial in maintaining proper kidney function and preventing dehydration, especially during warmer months.

4. **Natural and Whole Foods**: Fresh foods are minimally processed and closer to their natural state, providing a wholesome and nutritious option for your Budgie. Whole foods offer additional benefits such as dietary fiber for digestive health and antioxidants for immune support.

Commercial Diets:

1. **Convenience and Consistency**: Commercial diets, such as seeds and pellets, offer convenience and consistency in feeding. They provide a balanced blend of essential nutrients in every bite, ensuring that your

Budgie receives a consistent level of nutrition with minimal effort.

2. **Nutrient Fortification**: Commercial diets are often fortified with vitamins, minerals, and other essential nutrients to meet the specific dietary requirements of Budgerigars. This helps ensure that your Budgie receives all the necessary nutrients for optimal health and well-being.

3. **Long Shelf Life**: Commercial diets have a longer shelf life compared to fresh foods, making them convenient for storage and use. This can be particularly advantageous if you have limited access to fresh produce or prefer to stock up on food supplies in advance.

4. **Controlled Portions**: Commercial diets allow for precise portion control, making it easier to monitor your Budgie's food intake and prevent overeating or selective feeding. This can help maintain a healthy weight and reduce the risk of obesity-related health issues.

Finding the Right Balance:

Ultimately, the ideal diet for your Budgerigar is a combination of both fresh foods and commercial diets. By offering a balanced mix of seeds, pellets, fresh fruits, and vegetables, you can provide your Budgie with a diverse and nutritious diet that meets all of their nutritional needs.

Consider consulting with an avian veterinarian or a qualified avian nutritionist to develop a customized diet plan tailored to your Budgie's specific needs and preferences. Regularly monitor your Budgie's health, weight, and overall condition, and adjust their diet as necessary to ensure optimal health and well-being. With the right balance of fresh foods and commercial diets, you'll provide your Budgie with the best possible nutrition for a long and healthy life.

Safe and Unsafe Foods for Budgerigars

Knowing which foods are safe and which should be avoided is essential for maintaining your Budgerigar's health and well-being. While Budgies can enjoy a variety of fresh fruits, vegetables, and other foods, some items can be harmful or even toxic to them. Here's a comprehensive list of safe and unsafe foods for Budgerigars:

Safe Foods:

1. **Fruits**: Apples (seeds removed), bananas, berries (e.g., strawberries, blueberries, raspberries), grapes

(seedless), melons (e.g., watermelon, cantaloupe), oranges (in small amounts, without seeds), and pears.

2. **Vegetables**: Broccoli, carrots, cucumbers, bell peppers (all colors), leafy greens (e.g., spinach, kale, Swiss chard), peas, squash (e.g., zucchini, pumpkin), and sweet potatoes (cooked).

3. **Protein Sources**: Cooked eggs (hard-boiled or scrambled), cooked lean meats (e.g., chicken, turkey), cooked legumes (e.g., lentils, chickpeas), and tofu (plain, without seasoning).

4. **Grains and Seeds**: Cooked rice, cooked quinoa, whole grains (e.g., millet, barley), and small amounts of unsalted nuts and seeds (e.g., sunflower seeds, pumpkin seeds).

5. **Herbs and Spices**: Basil, cilantro, dill, parsley, and small amounts of cinnamon or turmeric (plain, without added sugar or salt).

6. **Treats and Supplements**: Cuttlebone, mineral blocks, and commercial Budgie treats made specifically for birds (e.g., millet sprays, seed sticks).

Unsafe Foods:

1. **Avocado**: Contains a substance called persin, which is toxic to birds and can cause respiratory distress, weakness, and death.

2. **Chocolate**: Contains theobromine and caffeine, which are toxic to birds and can cause vomiting, diarrhea, seizures, and death.

3. **Caffeine**: Found in coffee, tea, and energy drinks, caffeine can cause cardiac arrhythmias, seizures, and death in birds.

4. **Alcohol**: Even small amounts of alcohol can cause respiratory depression, neurological symptoms, and death in birds.

5. **Salty Foods**: High-sodium foods such as chips, pretzels, and processed snacks can lead to dehydration, kidney damage, and electrolyte imbalances in birds.

6. **High-Fat Foods**: Fatty foods such as fried foods, fatty meats, and greasy snacks can contribute to obesity, liver disease, and other health issues in birds.

7. **Sugary Foods**: Foods high in sugar, such as candy, soda, and sugary cereals, can lead to obesity, diabetes, and dental problems in birds.

8. **Raw Beans and Legumes**: Raw beans contain toxins such as lectins and enzyme inhibitors, which can cause digestive upset and poisoning in birds. Always cook beans thoroughly before feeding them to your Budgie.

9. **Moldy or Spoiled Foods**: Moldy or spoiled foods can contain harmful toxins and bacteria that can cause digestive upset, illness, and even death in birds. Always ensure that fruits, vegetables, and other perishable foods are fresh and free from mold or spoilage before feeding them to your Budgie.

By feeding your Budgerigar a balanced diet consisting of safe and nutritious foods, you'll help ensure their health and well-being for years to come. Always monitor your Budgie's reaction to new foods, and consult with an avian veterinarian if you have any concerns about their diet or health.

Water Requirements

Water is essential for the health and well-being of Budgerigars, just like any other living creature. Providing access to clean, fresh water is crucial for maintaining hydration, aiding digestion, regulating body temperature, and supporting overall health. Here's what you need to know about water requirements for Budgerigars:

1. **Access to Fresh Water**: Ensure that your Budgerigar has access to clean, fresh water at all times. Change the water in their dish daily to prevent bacterial growth and contamination. Budgies may also enjoy bathing in their water dish, so make sure it's large enough for them to splash around comfortably.

2. **Water Dispenser or Bottle**: Consider using a water dispenser or bottle instead of a dish to provide water for your Budgie. These devices help prevent contamination and spillage, ensuring that the water remains clean and accessible throughout the day.

3. **Hydration Needs**: Budgerigars have relatively high metabolic rates and can become dehydrated quickly, especially in warm or dry environments. Monitor your Budgie's water intake and behavior to ensure they are drinking enough water to stay hydrated.

4. **Environmental Factors**: Factors such as temperature, humidity, and diet can affect your Budgie's water requirements. During hot weather or times of increased activity, your Budgie may need more water to stay hydrated. Likewise, feeding a diet

high in dry foods (such as seeds) may increase water consumption.

5. **Water Quality**: Use clean, fresh tap water or filtered water for your Budgie. Avoid using water that contains additives such as chlorine or fluoride, as these can be harmful to birds. If you're unsure about the quality of your tap water, consider using filtered or bottled water instead.

6. **Water Monitoring**: Keep an eye on your Budgie's water intake and behavior. Signs of dehydration include lethargy, loss of appetite, dry skin or beak, and reduced activity. If you notice any of these signs, encourage your Budgie to drink more water and consider consulting with a veterinarian.

7. **Travel and Transport**: When traveling with your Budgie, ensure they have access to water throughout the journey. Use a spill-proof water dispenser or bottle attached securely to their travel carrier to prevent spills and keep them hydrated during transit.

5 | BUDGERIGAR HEALTH AND WELLNESS

Signs of a Healthy Budgerigar

Ensuring the health and wellness of your Budgerigar is essential for their happiness and longevity. By familiarizing yourself with the signs of a healthy Budgie, you'll be better equipped to detect any changes or potential issues early on. Here are some key indicators of a healthy Budgerigar:

1. **Active Behavior**: A healthy Budgerigar is typically active, alert, and engaged in their surroundings. They will move around their cage freely, explore their environment, and interact with toys and perches.

2. **Bright Eyes**: Bright, clear eyes are a sign of good health in Budgerigars. The eyes should be free from discharge, swelling, or redness. Healthy Budgies will also exhibit a curious and attentive gaze.

3. **Smooth Feathers**: Healthy Budgerigars have smooth, sleek feathers that lie flat against their body. Their plumage should be clean, glossy, and free from any signs of molting, bald patches, or abnormal feather loss.

4. **Eating and Drinking**: A healthy Budgerigar will have a healthy appetite and eagerly consume food and water throughout the day. They should show interest in various food items and readily drink water from their dish or dispenser.

5. **Vocalization**: Budgies are naturally vocal birds and will produce a variety of chirps, tweets, and sounds throughout the day. A healthy Budgerigar will vocalize regularly, expressing contentment, curiosity, and social interaction.

6. **Proper Breathing**: Healthy Budgerigars breathe quietly and effortlessly, with no audible wheezing, rasping, or labored breathing. Their breathing should be steady and unobstructed, with no signs of respiratory distress.

7. **Normal Droppings**: Normal Budgerigar droppings consist of three components: solid feces, urates (white or cream-colored), and urine (clear or slightly cloudy). The feces should be firm and well-formed, with a distinct separation between the feces and urates.

8. **Maintaining Weight**: A healthy Budgerigar will maintain a stable weight within a normal range for their age and size. Regular monitoring of their weight

can help detect changes that may indicate health issues.

9. **Active Social Interaction**: Budgies are social creatures that thrive on interaction with their human caregivers and fellow Budgies. A healthy Budgerigar will engage in social activities such as preening, playing, and vocalizing with companions.

10. **Grooming Behavior**: Budgerigars regularly preen and groom themselves to maintain their feathers and overall appearance. They will use their beak to groom their feathers, remove debris, and keep their plumage in good condition.

Regular observation and interaction with your Budgerigar will help you become familiar with their normal behaviors and appearance, making it easier to identify any deviations or signs of illness. If you notice any concerning changes in your Budgie's health or behavior, consult with an avian veterinarian promptly for a thorough examination and appropriate treatment. By staying vigilant and proactive about your Budgie's health, you can help them lead a happy, healthy, and fulfilling life.

Common Health Issues and Diseases

While Budgerigars are generally hardy and resilient birds, they are still susceptible to a variety of health issues and diseases. Understanding the common health issues that affect Budgerigars can help you recognize symptoms early and seek prompt veterinary care. Here are some of the most common health issues and diseases seen in Budgerigars:

1. **Respiratory Infections**: Budgerigars are prone to respiratory infections caused by bacteria, viruses, or fungi. Symptoms may include sneezing, nasal discharge, wheezing, labored breathing, and tail bobbing. Respiratory infections can be serious and require veterinary treatment with antibiotics or antifungal medications.

2. **Parasites**: Budgerigars can be affected by external parasites such as mites and lice, as well as internal parasites like worms. Signs of parasitic infestation may include feather plucking, scratching, skin irritation, weight loss, and lethargy. Treatment typically involves parasiticides prescribed by a veterinarian.

3. **Gastrointestinal Issues**: Budgerigars are prone to digestive problems such as crop impaction, diarrhea,

and bacterial or yeast overgrowth in the digestive tract. Symptoms may include regurgitation, vomiting, changes in droppings, loss of appetite, and abdominal distension. Treatment may involve dietary adjustments, medication, and supportive care.

4. **Liver Disease**: Budgerigars are susceptible to liver disease, often caused by a diet high in fatty foods, toxins, or medications. Symptoms may include lethargy, loss of appetite, weight loss, and changes in droppings. Treatment may involve dietary changes, supportive care, and medications to support liver function.

5. **Vitamin and Mineral Deficiencies**: Budgerigars may develop deficiencies in essential vitamins and minerals, such as vitamin A, calcium, and iodine. Symptoms vary depending on the specific deficiency but may include poor feather quality, skeletal abnormalities, reproductive issues, and immune system suppression. Treatment involves supplementation and dietary adjustments.

6. **Tumors and Growths**: Budgerigars can develop tumors and growths, both benign and malignant, in various parts of the body. Common locations include

the skin, reproductive organs, and internal organs. Symptoms may include lumps or swellings, changes in behavior or activity level, and difficulty breathing or moving. Treatment depends on the type and location of the tumor and may involve surgical removal, chemotherapy, or supportive care.

7. **Egg Binding**: Female Budgerigars may experience egg binding, where an egg becomes stuck in the reproductive tract and cannot be laid naturally. Egg binding is a medical emergency and can be life-threatening if not treated promptly. Symptoms include straining, abdominal distension, and lethargy. Treatment involves gentle manipulation, supportive care, and sometimes surgery to remove the egg.

8. **Stress-Related Conditions**: Budgerigars are sensitive birds that can be prone to stress-related conditions such as feather plucking, self-mutilation, and behavioral disorders. Stressors may include changes in environment, social isolation, inadequate diet, and loud noises. Treatment involves identifying and addressing the underlying cause of stress, along with environmental enrichment and behavioral modification.

Regular Veterinary Check-ups

Just like any other pet, Budgerigars benefit greatly from regular veterinary check-ups. These routine visits are essential for monitoring their health, detecting any potential issues early on, and ensuring they receive appropriate care and treatment. Here's why regular veterinary check-ups are important for Budgerigars:

1. **Preventive Care**: Regular check-ups allow your avian veterinarian to assess your Budgie's overall health and identify any underlying issues before they become serious. Preventive care measures such as vaccinations, parasite control, and dietary recommendations can help keep your Budgie healthy and happy.

2. **Early Detection of Health Problems**: Budgerigars are masters at hiding signs of illness, which can make it challenging for owners to detect health problems. During a check-up, your veterinarian will perform a thorough physical examination, looking for signs of disease or abnormalities that may not be apparent to you. Early detection allows for prompt intervention and treatment, improving the prognosis for your Budgie.

3. **Nutritional Assessment**: Your veterinarian can provide valuable advice on your Budgie's diet and nutritional needs during a check-up. They can recommend appropriate foods, supplements, and feeding practices to ensure your Budgie receives a balanced diet that meets their specific requirements.

4. **Behavioral Evaluation**: Changes in behavior can be indicative of underlying health issues or environmental stressors. Your veterinarian can assess your Budgie's behavior during a check-up and offer guidance on addressing any behavioral concerns. They can also provide enrichment ideas to keep your Budgie mentally stimulated and engaged.

5. **Dental and Beak Health**: Budgerigars' beaks and teeth continuously grow throughout their lives, and issues such as overgrowth or malocclusion can lead to discomfort and difficulty eating. Your veterinarian can examine your Budgie's beak and oral cavity during a check-up and recommend appropriate dental care measures if necessary.

6. **Wing and Nail Trimming**: Regular wing and nail trimming may be necessary to prevent injuries and maintain your Budgie's mobility. Your veterinarian

can perform these procedures safely and effectively during a check-up, ensuring your Budgie remains comfortable and well-groomed.

7. **Establishing a Relationship with Your Veterinarian**: Regular check-ups allow you to establish a relationship with your avian veterinarian, who can become familiar with your Budgie's unique needs and health history. This relationship fosters trust and ensures that you have a reliable resource for advice and support regarding your Budgie's care.

Schedule regular veterinary check-ups for your Budgerigar at least once a year, or more frequently if recommended by your veterinarian. During these visits, be sure to discuss any concerns or questions you may have about your Budgie's health or behavior.

First Aid and Emergency Care

Being prepared to provide first aid and emergency care for your Budgerigar is essential for their health and well-being. While Budgies are relatively hardy birds, accidents and emergencies can still occur. Here's a guide to help you handle common emergencies and provide basic first aid for your Budgerigar:

1. Handling an Injured Budgerigar:

- Approach your Budgie calmly and gently to avoid causing further stress or injury.

- Use a towel or cloth to carefully pick up your Budgie, supporting their body and wings.

- Place your Budgie in a small, secure carrier or box lined with soft bedding for transport to the veterinarian.

2. Bleeding:

- If your Budgie is bleeding from a wound, apply gentle pressure with a clean cloth or gauze to stop the bleeding.

- Avoid using cotton balls or fibers that can stick to the wound and cause further injury.

- Seek veterinary attention promptly for assessment and treatment of the wound.

3. Respiratory Distress:

- If your Budgie is experiencing difficulty breathing or respiratory distress, move them to a quiet, warm, and well-ventilated area.

- Avoid exposing your Budgie to drafts, smoke, or strong odors that can exacerbate respiratory symptoms.

- Seek immediate veterinary care for evaluation and treatment of respiratory issues.

4. Choking:

- If your Budgie is choking on a foreign object, remain calm and assess the situation carefully.

- If the object is visible and easily reachable, gently attempt to remove it with tweezers or your fingers.

- If the object cannot be safely removed, seek veterinary assistance immediately.

5. Heat Stress:

- Budgerigars are sensitive to high temperatures and can suffer from heat stress or heatstroke.

- Move your Budgie to a cool, shaded area and offer them fresh water to drink.

- Use a spray bottle to mist your Budgie with cool water or place a damp cloth over their cage to help lower their body temperature.

- Monitor your Budgie closely for signs of improvement or worsening symptoms and seek veterinary care if necessary.

6. Seizures:

- If your Budgie is having a seizure, remove any objects or obstacles from their immediate vicinity to prevent injury.

- Keep the area quiet and dimly lit to minimize stimulation.

- Do not attempt to restrain your Budgie during a seizure, as this can cause further stress or injury.

- Time the duration of the seizure and seek veterinary attention if seizures persist or recur.

7. Poisoning:

- If you suspect your Budgie has ingested a toxic substance, contact your veterinarian or a poison control hotline immediately for guidance.

- Provide as much information as possible about the suspected toxin, including the type of substance ingested and the quantity.

- Follow any instructions provided by your veterinarian or poison control specialist for managing poisoning emergencies.

8. Transportation:

- When transporting your Budgie to the veterinarian, use a small, secure carrier or box lined with soft bedding to minimize stress and prevent further injury.

- Ensure adequate ventilation and avoid sudden movements or jostling during transport.

- Keep the carrier covered with a light cloth or towel to provide privacy and reduce stress for your Budgie.

9. Veterinary Contact Information:

- Keep the contact information for your avian veterinarian readily accessible in case of emergencies.

- Familiarize yourself with their hours of operation and emergency procedures, including after-hours and weekend care options.

10. Preparation:

- Consider assembling a basic first aid kit for your Budgerigar, including items such as gauze pads, adhesive bandages, styptic powder, a small carrier or box, and contact information for your veterinarian.

Being prepared to handle emergencies and provide first aid for your Budgerigar can make a critical difference in their outcome. Stay calm, act quickly, and seek veterinary assistance as soon as possible for the best chance of a positive outcome.

6 | BEHAVIORAL ASPECTS OF BUDGERIGARS

Bonding with Your Budgerigar

Building a strong bond with your Budgerigar is key to fostering a trusting and rewarding relationship. Budgies are intelligent and social birds that thrive on interaction and companionship, and forming a close bond with them enhances their overall well-being. Here are some tips to help you bond with your Budgerigar:

1. **Respect Their Space**: Allow your Budgerigar to acclimate to their new environment at their own pace. Avoid overwhelming them with too much attention or handling during the initial adjustment period.

2. **Patience and Consistency**: Building trust takes time and patience. Spend time with your Budgerigar regularly, talking to them softly and offering treats from your hand. Be consistent in your interactions and routines to establish a sense of security and predictability.

3. **Positive Reinforcement**: Use positive reinforcement techniques such as praise, treats, and gentle petting to reward desired behaviors. Encourage your Budgie to approach you willingly by offering treats or favorite toys as incentives.

4. **Hand Taming**: Gradually introduce your hand into your Budgie's space, allowing them to become accustomed to your presence without feeling threatened. Offer treats from your fingers or a flat palm to encourage them to approach and explore your hand.

5. **Respect Their Boundaries**: Pay attention to your Budgie's body language and vocalizations to gauge their comfort level. If they show signs of fear or discomfort, back off and give them space. Respect their boundaries and avoid forcing interactions.

6. **Mutual Activities**: Engage in activities that your Budgie enjoys, such as playing with toys, exploring new perches, or listening to music together. Spending quality time together strengthens your bond and enhances your Budgie's sense of companionship.

7. **Training Sessions**: Incorporate short training sessions into your bonding routine to stimulate your

Budgie's mind and reinforce positive behaviors. Teach them simple tricks or commands using positive reinforcement methods to build trust and confidence.

8. **Be Patient and Understanding**: Every Budgie is unique, and bonding progress may vary from bird to bird. Be patient and understanding, respecting your Budgie's individual personality and preferences. Celebrate small victories and milestones along the way.

9. **Respect Their Independence**: While building a bond with your Budgie is important, it's also essential to respect their need for independence and autonomy. Allow them time alone to rest, preen, and engage in natural behaviors without constant interaction.

10. **Consistent Care and Routine**: Establish a consistent care routine that includes regular feeding, cleaning, and social interaction. Consistency and predictability create a sense of security and stability for your Budgie, strengthening your bond over time.

Understanding Budgerigar Communication

Budgerigars, like many other birds, communicate through a combination of vocalizations, body language, and behaviors. Understanding their unique communication cues is essential for interpreting their needs, emotions, and interactions within their social group. Here's a guide to help you decipher and respond to Budgerigar communication:

1. Vocalizations:

- **Chirping and Singing:** Budgerigars are known for their melodious chirps and songs, which serve various purposes such as socializing, expressing contentment, and communicating with flock members.

- **Contact Calls:** Budgies use contact calls to maintain communication with their flock members, even when they're out of sight. These short, repetitive chirps help them stay connected and alert to each other's presence.

- **Alarm Calls:** Loud, sharp chirps or screeches may indicate distress, fear, or alarm. Pay attention to the context of the alarm call and investigate for potential threats or stressors in the environment.

2. Body Language:

- **Fluffed Feathers:** Fluffing up their feathers can indicate relaxation, contentment, or readiness for sleep. However, it can also be a sign of illness or discomfort, so observe your Budgie's overall behavior and appearance for context.

- **Head Bobbing:** Rapid head bobbing, often accompanied by chirping or vocalizations, is a common display of excitement, enthusiasm, or courtship behavior in Budgerigars.

- **Wing Fluttering:** Rapid fluttering of the wings, especially when accompanied by vocalizations and dancing movements, may indicate happiness, anticipation, or a desire for attention.

3. Behaviors:

- **Exploration:** Budgies are curious and inquisitive birds that enjoy exploring their surroundings. They may investigate new toys, perches, or objects in their environment as a form of enrichment and stimulation.

- **Playfulness:** Budgerigars engage in playful behaviors such as hopping, jumping, and climbing, especially when they're feeling energetic and sociable. Providing a variety of toys and activities can encourage playful behavior and mental stimulation.

- **Social Interactions:** Budgies are highly social birds that thrive on interaction with their human caregivers and fellow Budgies. They may engage in mutual preening, beak tapping, or other forms of social bonding to strengthen relationships within their flock.

4. Response and Interaction:

- **Observation:** Pay close attention to your Budgie's vocalizations, body language, and behaviors to gauge their mood, needs, and preferences. Each Budgie has a unique communication style, so take the time to learn and understand your Budgie's individual cues.

- **Responsive Interaction:** Respond to your Budgie's vocalizations and behaviors with gentle, positive reinforcement. Engage in interactive play, offer treats, and provide verbal praise to reinforce desired behaviors and strengthen your bond.

Training and Socialization Techniques

Training and socialization are important aspects of Budgerigar care that help foster positive behaviors, strengthen the bond between you and your bird, and enhance their overall well-being. With patience, consistency, and positive reinforcement, you can teach your Budgie new skills, encourage social interactions, and create a stimulating environment for them to thrive. Here are some effective training and socialization techniques for Budgerigars:

1. Hand Taming:

- **Gradual Approach:** Begin by gradually introducing your hand into your Budgie's environment, allowing them to become accustomed to your presence without feeling threatened.

- **Positive Reinforcement:** Use treats, praise, and gentle petting to reward your Budgie for approaching your hand voluntarily. Associate your hand with positive experiences to build trust and confidence.

- **Slow Progression:** Proceed at your Budgie's pace, gradually increasing the proximity and duration of hand interactions. Avoid rushing or forcing physical contact, as this can undermine trust and lead to fearfulness.

2. Target Training:

- **Target Stick:** Introduce a target stick (such as a chopstick or dowel) and use it to guide your Budgie to touch a designated target, such as a small bead or sticker.

- **Positive Reinforcement:** Reward your Budgie with treats or praise each time they successfully touch the target with their beak. Repeat the exercise regularly to reinforce the desired behavior.

- **Progression:** Gradually increase the distance and complexity of the target training exercises, encouraging your Budgie to follow the target stick to different locations or perform specific actions.

3. Step-Up Training:

- **Perch or Finger:** Encourage your Budgie to step onto a perch or your finger by offering a treat as a reward. Use a verbal cue such as "step up" to signal the desired behavior.

- **Positive Reinforcement:** Reward your Budgie with treats and praise each time they successfully step onto the perch or your finger. Repeat the exercise consistently to reinforce the step-up behavior.

- **Consistency:** Practice step-up training regularly to build your Budgie's confidence and responsiveness to the cue. Be patient and supportive, providing encouragement and reinforcement as needed.

4. Socialization:

- **Group Interaction:** Allow your Budgie to interact with other Budgies in a supervised and controlled environment. Socialization with flock mates helps promote natural behaviors, social skills, and mental stimulation.

- **Human Interaction:** Spend quality time interacting with your Budgie daily, engaging in activities such as talking, singing, and playing together. Offer treats, toys, and positive reinforcement to strengthen your bond and encourage socialization.

- **Enrichment Activities:** Provide a variety of toys, perches, and environmental stimuli to keep your Budgie mentally stimulated and engaged. Rotate toys regularly to prevent boredom and encourage exploration and play.

5. Consistency and Patience:

- **Consistent Training:** Practice training and socialization techniques consistently, incorporating short sessions into your daily routine. Consistency is key to reinforcing desired behaviors and building trust and confidence.

- **Patience:** Be patient and understanding, allowing your Budgie time to learn and adjust to new experiences at their own pace. Celebrate small successes and progress, and avoid becoming discouraged by setbacks or challenges.

Dealing with Behavioral Problems in Budgerigars

While Budgerigars are generally social and well-behaved pets, they may occasionally exhibit behavioral problems that require attention and intervention. Understanding the underlying causes of these behaviors and implementing appropriate strategies can help address and resolve issues effectively. Here are some common behavioral problems in Budgerigars and how to deal with them:

1. Feather Plucking:

- **Causes:** Feather plucking can be caused by various factors, including stress, boredom, medical conditions, or environmental factors.

- **Intervention:** Identify and address any underlying causes of stress or discomfort, such as inadequate cage size, lack of mental stimulation, or improper diet. Provide environmental enrichment, social interaction, and regular veterinary check-ups to promote healthy feather growth and discourage plucking behavior.

2. Aggression:

- **Causes:** Aggression in Budgerigars may stem from territorial disputes, fear, hormonal changes, or lack of socialization.

- **Intervention:** Address the root cause of aggression by providing a spacious and well-structured environment, minimizing stressors, and promoting positive social interactions. Use positive reinforcement techniques to encourage calm and non-aggressive behavior, and avoid punishing or reinforcing aggressive responses.

3. Excessive Vocalization:

- **Causes:** Excessive vocalization, such as loud chirping or squawking, may indicate boredom, loneliness, or territorial behavior.

- **Intervention:** Provide mental and physical stimulation through interactive toys, social interaction, and environmental enrichment. Establish a consistent daily routine to promote a sense of security and stability. Avoid reinforcing vocalization by responding to excessive noise with attention or treats, as this may inadvertently reinforce the behavior.

4. Territorial Behavior:

- **Causes:** Territorial behavior, such as aggression towards other birds or objects, may occur in response to perceived threats or changes in the environment.

- **Intervention:** Identify and minimize triggers for territorial behavior, such as new cage mates, changes in cage layout, or introduction of unfamiliar objects. Use positive reinforcement to encourage calm and cooperative behavior, and provide ample space and resources to reduce competition and conflict.

5. Fear and Shyness:

- **Causes:** Fear and shyness in Budgerigars may result from past trauma, lack of socialization, or genetic predisposition.

- **Intervention:** Create a safe and secure environment for your Budgie, minimizing sudden noises, movements, and changes. Gradually desensitize your Budgie to fearful stimuli through gradual exposure and positive reinforcement. Build trust and confidence through patient and gentle interaction, respecting your Budgie's comfort zone and boundaries.

6. Destructive Behavior:

- **Causes:** Destructive behavior, such as chewing on cage bars or shredding toys, may stem from boredom, lack of stimulation, or excess energy.

- **Intervention:** Provide a variety of safe and appropriate chew toys, foraging opportunities, and enrichment activities to redirect destructive behavior. Ensure that your Budgie receives regular exercise and mental stimulation to channel their energy productively.

7. Excessive Nesting Behavior:

- **Causes:** Excessive nesting behavior, such as compulsive nest building or egg laying, may be triggered by hormonal changes, breeding instincts, or environmental factors.

- **Intervention:** Minimize hormonal triggers by providing a consistent light cycle, avoiding excessive handling or petting, and removing potential nesting materials from the cage. Consult with a veterinarian to address hormonal imbalances or reproductive issues if necessary.

When dealing with behavioral problems in Budgerigars, it's important to approach the situation with patience, understanding, and a proactive mindset. By identifying and addressing the underlying causes of problematic behaviors and implementing appropriate intervention strategies, you can help your Budgie overcome challenges and lead a happy, healthy, and well-adjusted life as part of your family. If behavioral problems persist or worsen despite your efforts, consult with a qualified avian veterinarian or behavior specialist for additional guidance and support.

7 | ENRICHMENT AND ENTERTAINMENT

Providing Mental Stimulation

Mental stimulation is essential for the well-being and happiness of Budgerigars. As intelligent and curious birds, Budgies thrive on mental challenges and enrichment activities that engage their natural instincts and behaviors. By providing opportunities for mental stimulation, you can help prevent boredom, encourage exploration, and enhance your Budgie's overall quality of life. Here are some effective ways to provide mental stimulation for your Budgerigar:

1. **Interactive Toys:** Offer a variety of interactive toys that encourage exploration, problem-solving, and physical activity. Toys such as puzzle feeders, foraging toys, and bells provide mental challenges and opportunities for play.

2. **Rotate Toys Regularly:** Rotate your Budgie's toys regularly to keep their environment interesting and prevent boredom. Introduce new toys periodically to maintain novelty and stimulate their curiosity.

3. **Natural Materials:** Incorporate natural materials such as untreated wood, bamboo, and seagrass into

your Budgie's environment. These materials provide safe and engaging surfaces for chewing, shredding, and exploration.

4. **Mirror Play:** Provide a small, safe mirror in your Budgie's cage to encourage social interaction and vocalization. Budgies often enjoy interacting with their own reflection, which can provide mental stimulation and companionship.

5. **Training Sessions:** Engage in short training sessions with your Budgie to teach them simple tricks or commands using positive reinforcement techniques. Training sessions stimulate their cognitive abilities, strengthen the bond between you and your Budgie, and provide mental enrichment.

6. **Environmental Enrichment:** Create a stimulating environment for your Budgie by adding perches of different shapes and sizes, natural branches for climbing, and hiding spots for exploration. Arrange cage furnishings to encourage movement and activity.

7. **Audio and Visual Stimulation:** Play soft music or nature sounds in the background to provide auditory stimulation for your Budgie. You can also hang

colorful, visually stimulating toys or decorations near their cage to capture their interest.

8. **Outdoor Time:** Allow your Budgie supervised outdoor time in a secure and enclosed area, such as a screened porch or aviary. Exposure to natural sunlight, fresh air, and different sights and sounds provides valuable mental stimulation and sensory enrichment.

9. **Social Interaction:** Budgerigars are social birds that benefit from interaction with their human caregivers and fellow Budgies. Spend quality time talking, singing, and playing with your Budgie to provide mental stimulation and companionship.

10. **Food Enrichment:** Offer a variety of fresh fruits, vegetables, and healthy treats in different textures and shapes to stimulate your Budgie's senses and encourage foraging behavior. Hide treats in foraging toys or scatter them throughout their cage to promote natural feeding behaviors

Toys and Activities for Budgerigars

Providing a variety of toys and activities is essential for keeping Budgerigars mentally stimulated, physically active, and emotionally fulfilled. Budgies are intelligent and curious birds that enjoy exploring their environment, interacting with toys, and engaging in play. Here are some recommended toys and activities to enrich your Budgerigar's life:

1. **Interactive Toys:**

    - **Puzzle Feeders:** Fill puzzle feeders with treats or seeds to encourage foraging behavior and problem-solving skills.

    - **Foraging Toys:** Hide treats or food items inside foraging toys, encouraging Budgies to search for and retrieve their rewards.

    - **Rolling Balls:** Provide rolling balls or toys with bells inside for Budgies to push and chase, stimulating both physical and mental activity.

2. **Chew Toys:**

    - **Wooden Blocks:** Offer untreated wooden blocks or branches for Budgies to chew on, helping to satisfy their natural urge to gnaw and maintain healthy beak condition.

- **Mineral Blocks:** Provide mineral blocks or cuttlebones to supplement your Budgie's diet with essential minerals and encourage chewing behavior.

3. **Swinging and Climbing Toys:**

- **Swings:** Hang swings of various sizes and shapes for Budgies to perch on and swing back and forth, providing physical exercise and entertainment.

- **Ladders:** Install ladders or rope perches in the cage to encourage climbing and exploration, mimicking their natural habitat and promoting agility.

4. **Mirrors and Reflection Toys:**

- **Mirrors:** Place small, safe mirrors inside the cage to stimulate social interaction and vocalization, allowing Budgies to interact with their own reflection.

- **Reflective Objects:** Hang shiny or reflective objects, such as bells or metallic toys, to capture Budgies' attention and encourage play.

5. **Interactive and Training Activities:**

   - **Target Training:** Teach Budgies simple tricks or commands using target training techniques, rewarding them with treats for desired behaviors.

   - **Interactive Games:** Play interactive games with your Budgie, such as "fetch" with a small toy or "hide and seek" with treats hidden around the cage.

6. **Natural Materials and DIY Toys:**

   - **Natural Branches:** Provide natural branches or perches of varying textures and diameters for Budgies to perch on and chew, promoting foot health and exercise.

   - **DIY Toys:** Create homemade toys using safe materials such as paper, cardboard, and natural fibers, encouraging Budgies to shred and explore.

7. **Rotation and Variety:**

- **Rotate Toys:** Rotate and replace toys regularly to prevent boredom and maintain your Budgie's interest in their environment.

- **Variety:** Offer a variety of toys with different textures, shapes, and functions to cater to your Budgie's preferences and stimulate their curiosity.

8. **Supervised Outdoor Time:**

- **Outdoor Aviary:** Provide supervised outdoor time in a secure and enclosed outdoor aviary or screened porch, allowing Budgies to experience natural sunlight, fresh air, and different sights and sounds.

Safe Out-of-Cage Time

Allowing Budgerigars to have supervised out-of-cage time is an excellent way to promote exercise, mental stimulation, and social interaction. However, it's essential to ensure their safety and well-being during these periods of freedom. Here are some guidelines for providing safe out-of-cage time for your Budgerigars:

1. **Secure the Area:** Before letting your Budgerigars out of their cage, ensure that the room is safe and secure. Close all windows and doors to prevent escapes, and eliminate any potential hazards such as open containers of water, electrical cords, or toxic plants.

2. **Supervision:** Always supervise your Budgerigars closely during out-of-cage time to prevent accidents and monitor their behavior. Keep an eye on them at all times and intervene if they show signs of distress or engage in unsafe activities.

3. **Limit Access:** Restrict your Budgerigars' access to high-risk areas such as kitchens, bathrooms, and areas with open flames or appliances. Block off access to any areas where they could get trapped or injured.

4. **Provide Perches:** Place perches or play stands in the out-of-cage area to give your Budgerigars a place to perch, rest, and explore. Ensure that the perches are stable and secure to prevent accidents or falls.

5. **Toys and Activities:** Offer toys, puzzles, and interactive activities to keep your Budgerigars mentally stimulated and entertained during out-of-

cage time. Rotate toys regularly to maintain their interest and prevent boredom.

6. **Flight Training:** If your Budgerigars are fully flighted, consider implementing flight training exercises during out-of-cage time. Encourage them to fly short distances between perches or targets, gradually increasing the distance as they become more confident.

7. **Bathroom Breaks:** Keep a close watch on your Budgerigars' behavior and provide opportunities for bathroom breaks as needed. Place newspaper or absorbent pads in designated areas to facilitate clean-up and minimize mess.

8. **Return to Cage:** When out-of-cage time is over, gently encourage your Budgerigars to return to their cage using positive reinforcement techniques such as offering treats or verbal cues. Avoid chasing or forcing them back into the cage, as this can cause stress and reluctance to come out in the future.

9. **Regular Exercise:** Aim for regular, daily out-of-cage time to provide your Budgerigars with ample opportunities for exercise, exploration, and socialization. Gradually increase the duration of out-

of-cage sessions as your Budgerigars become more accustomed to the routine.

10. **Emergency Preparedness:** Be prepared for emergencies by keeping a first aid kit, including items such as styptic powder, bandages, and a bird-safe disinfectant, readily available. Know the location of your nearest avian veterinarian and have their contact information on hand in case of emergencies.

8 | BREEDING AND REPRODUCTION

Breeding Considerations

Breeding Budgerigars can be a rewarding experience, but it requires careful planning, preparation, and consideration of various factors to ensure the health and well-being of the breeding pair and their offspring. Before embarking on a breeding program, it's essential to understand the responsibilities and commitments involved. Here are some key considerations to keep in mind when breeding Budgerigars:

1. **Breeding Age:** Budgerigars typically reach sexual maturity around 6 to 8 months of age, although individual birds may vary. It's important to wait until both the male and female Budgerigars are mature enough before attempting to breed them to avoid potential health risks and complications.

2. **Pair Compatibility:** Selecting compatible breeding pairs is crucial for successful reproduction. Consider factors such as age, temperament, and genetic compatibility when pairing Budgerigars. Avoid

breeding close relatives to minimize the risk of genetic abnormalities and health problems in the offspring.

3. **Health Screening:** Ensure that both the male and female Budgerigars are in optimal health before breeding. Schedule a pre-breeding health check-up with an avian veterinarian to assess their overall condition, detect any underlying health issues, and address any necessary vaccinations or treatments.

4. **Breeding Environment:** Provide a suitable breeding environment for your Budgerigars, including a spacious breeding cage or nest box with appropriate nesting materials such as shredded paper or wood shavings. Ensure that the breeding area is quiet, secure, and free from disturbances to minimize stress and promote successful breeding behavior.

5. **Nutrition and Diet:** Proper nutrition is essential for breeding Budgerigars. Provide a balanced diet consisting of high-quality seeds, pellets, fresh fruits, and vegetables to ensure optimal health and reproductive performance. Supplement their diet with calcium-rich foods such as cuttlebone or mineral blocks to support egg production and shell formation.

6. **Breeding Season:** Budgerigars are seasonal breeders, with the breeding season typically occurring during the warmer months of spring and summer. Provide appropriate lighting and environmental cues to simulate natural breeding conditions and encourage breeding behavior.

7. **Egg Laying and Incubation:** Female Budgerigars typically lay eggs every other day until they have laid a clutch of 4 to 6 eggs. Ensure that the breeding pair has access to a suitable nest box or breeding cage with adequate nesting materials for egg laying and incubation. Monitor the nest box regularly for signs of egg laying, and avoid disturbing the breeding pair during this critical period.

8. **Parental Care:** Both the male and female Budgerigars play important roles in caring for their offspring. Provide a supportive environment for the breeding pair, ensuring access to fresh food, water, and nesting materials throughout the breeding cycle. Monitor the parents' behavior closely to ensure they are feeding, incubating, and caring for the chicks properly.

9. **Hand-Rearing Considerations:** If you plan to hand-rear chicks, ensure that you have the necessary knowledge, experience, and resources to do so safely and responsibly. Hand-rearing requires round-the-clock care, specialized feeding formulas, and meticulous attention to detail to ensure the health and well-being of the chicks.

10. **Breeding Ethics:** Practice responsible breeding practices and prioritize the health and welfare of the breeding pair and their offspring. Avoid overbreeding or excessive breeding, and be prepared to provide lifelong care for any chicks that are not sold or adopted.

Nesting and Egg Incubation

Nesting and egg incubation are critical stages in the breeding process of Budgerigars. Proper nest preparation, egg laying, and incubation are essential for the health and development of the offspring. Here's what you need to know about nesting and egg incubation in Budgerigars:

1. **Nest Box Preparation:**

- Choose a suitable nest box that is appropriately sized for Budgerigars, with dimensions around 6-8 inches in length, width, and height.

- Line the bottom of the nest box with nesting materials such as shredded paper, wood shavings, or nesting fibers to provide a soft and comfortable substrate for the eggs.

- Place the nest box in a quiet and secluded area of the cage or aviary, away from disturbances and drafts, to provide a safe and secure environment for nesting.

2. **Egg Laying:**

- Female Budgerigars typically lay eggs every other day until they have completed a clutch of 4-6 eggs.

- Monitor the female closely for signs of egg laying, such as spending extended periods in the nest box, increased appetite, and changes in behavior.

- Provide a calcium supplement, such as a cuttlebone or mineral block, to support egg production and shell formation.

3. **Incubation Period:**

- Budgerigar eggs have an incubation period of approximately 18-21 days, during which the female will incubate the eggs continuously.

- Ensure that the nest box remains undisturbed during the incubation period to minimize stress and disruptions for the breeding pair.

- Monitor the nest box regularly to ensure that the eggs are being attended to and that the female is rotating them periodically for even incubation.

4. **Parental Care:**

- Both the male and female Budgerigars play important roles in caring for the eggs and chicks. The female is primarily responsible for incubating the eggs, while the male provides support by bringing food and other resources to the nest.

- Ensure that the breeding pair has access to a nutritious diet, fresh water, and nesting materials throughout the incubation period to support their parental duties.

5. **Egg Candling:**

- Egg candling is a technique used to assess the viability of developing embryos within the eggs. Shine a bright light source, such as a flashlight or candling lamp, through the egg to illuminate the contents.

- Monitor the development of the embryos by observing the presence of blood vessels and movement within the egg. Remove any infertile or non-viable eggs from the nest to prevent contamination and reduce the risk of infection.

6. **Hatching and Chick Care:**

- Budgerigar chicks typically hatch within a 24-48 hour period after the start of pip, the initial crack in the eggshell made by the chick's beak.

- Provide a warm and stable environment for the newly hatched chicks, ensuring access to food, water, and warmth from the parents.

- Monitor the health and development of the chicks closely, addressing any issues such as splay legs or feeding difficulties promptly to ensure their well-being.

Caring for Budgerigar Chicks

Caring for Budgerigar chicks requires careful attention, patience, and dedication to ensure their health, growth, and development. From hatching to fledging, Budgerigar chicks rely on their parents and caregivers for essential care and support. Here's how to provide optimal care for Budgerigar chicks:

1. **Nest Box Environment:**

   - Maintain a clean and hygienic nest box environment for the chicks, ensuring that nesting materials remain dry and free from contamination.

   - Monitor the temperature and humidity levels in the nest box to provide a comfortable and stable environment for the chicks' growth and development.

2. **Feeding and Nutrition:**

   - Budgerigar chicks are initially fed crop milk by their parents, a nutrient-rich secretion produced in the parent birds' crop glands.

- Ensure that the breeding pair has access to a nutritious diet of seeds, pellets, fresh fruits, and vegetables to support their ability to produce crop milk for the chicks.

- If hand-rearing chicks, provide a suitable hand-feeding formula designed for parrot chicks, following the manufacturer's instructions for mixing and feeding.

3. **Feeding Schedule:**

- Budgerigar chicks require frequent feedings throughout the day, typically every 2-3 hours during the first week of life.

- Monitor the chicks' crop to ensure that it empties completely between feedings and does not become impacted or distended, which can indicate overfeeding or feeding-related issues.

4. **Monitoring Growth and Development:**

- Monitor the growth and development of the chicks closely, assessing their weight, feather development, and overall condition regularly.

- Keep a record of each chick's progress, including weight measurements, feeding

schedule, and any observations of abnormal
behavior or health concerns.

5. **Socialization and Handling:**

- Handle the chicks gently and minimally to
  avoid causing stress or injury. Limit handling
  to essential tasks such as feeding, weighing,
  and health checks.

- Encourage socialization with human caregivers
  by spending time near the nest box and
  speaking softly to the chicks to familiarize them
  with human interaction.

6. **Weaning Process:**

- Budgerigar chicks begin the process of weaning
  at around 4-6 weeks of age, gradually
  transitioning from crop milk to solid foods.

- Offer softened pellets, seeds, and fresh fruits
  and vegetables in small, bite-sized pieces to
  encourage the chicks to explore and
  experiment with solid foods.

7. **Fledging and Flight Training:**

- Budgerigar chicks typically fledge, or leave the nest, between 4-6 weeks of age, although individual chicks may vary in their timing.

- Provide opportunities for fledgling chicks to exercise and strengthen their flight muscles by offering perches and encouraging short flights within a safe and supervised environment.

8. **Health Monitoring and Veterinary Care:**

- Monitor the health and well-being of the chicks closely, observing for any signs of illness, injury, or developmental abnormalities.

- Seek veterinary care promptly if you notice any concerns or abnormalities in the chicks' behavior, appetite, or physical condition.

9 | LONGEVITY AND END-OF-LIFE CARE

Budgerigar Lifespan

Understanding the lifespan of Budgerigars is essential for providing proper care and planning for their long-term well-being. Budgerigars are relatively long-lived birds compared to many other small parrot species, with an average lifespan of 5 to 10 years in captivity. However, with attentive care, a healthy diet, and a suitable environment, Budgerigars can live well beyond 10 years, with some individuals reaching 15 years or more.

Several factors can influence the lifespan of Budgerigars:

1. **Genetics:** Genetic factors play a significant role in determining the lifespan of Budgerigars. Birds from reputable breeders with a focus on breeding for health and longevity may have a better chance of living longer lives.

2. **Nutrition:** A balanced and nutritious diet is crucial for maintaining the health and longevity of Budgerigars. Providing a varied diet of high-quality seeds, pellets, fresh fruits, and vegetables ensures that

Budgerigars receive essential nutrients to support their overall health and immune function.

3. **Environment:** A clean, spacious, and stimulating environment contributes to the well-being of Budgerigars and can help extend their lifespan. Proper cage or aviary setup, regular cleaning, and access to fresh air and sunlight are essential for promoting longevity.

4. **Veterinary Care:** Regular veterinary check-ups and prompt treatment of any health issues or concerns can help prevent or address potential health problems that may affect Budgerigar lifespan. Routine examinations, vaccinations, and parasite control are essential components of preventive care.

5. **Socialization:** Budgerigars are social birds that thrive on interaction and companionship. Providing opportunities for socialization, mental stimulation, and enrichment activities can contribute to their overall happiness and longevity.

6. **Genetic Diseases:** Some Budgerigars may be predisposed to certain genetic diseases or health conditions that can affect their lifespan. Responsible

breeding practices and genetic screening can help reduce the risk of inherited health problems.

7. **Quality of Life:** Ensuring a high quality of life for Budgerigars, including access to proper nutrition, veterinary care, and social interaction, can have a significant impact on their lifespan and overall well-being.

Quality of Life Considerations

Ensuring a high quality of life for Budgerigars is essential for their overall well-being and longevity. Budgerigars, like all living creatures, have physical, emotional, and behavioral needs that must be met to thrive in captivity. Here are some key considerations for enhancing the quality of life for Budgerigars:

1. **Proper Housing and Environment:**

   - Provide a spacious and well-structured cage or aviary that allows Budgerigars to move freely, stretch their wings, and engage in natural behaviors such as perching, climbing, and flying short distances.

- Furnish the cage with a variety of perches, toys, and enrichment activities to stimulate physical activity, mental stimulation, and social interaction.

2. **Nutritious Diet:**

   - Offer a balanced and varied diet consisting of high-quality seeds, pellets, fresh fruits, and vegetables to meet the nutritional needs of Budgerigars. Supplement their diet with calcium-rich foods and vitamin supplements as needed to support their health and vitality.

3. **Social Interaction:**

   - Budgerigars are social birds that thrive on interaction and companionship. Spend quality time interacting with your Budgerigar through talking, singing, and gentle handling to strengthen the bond between you and promote their emotional well-being.

4. **Environmental Enrichment:**

   - Provide opportunities for mental stimulation and enrichment through the use of interactive toys, foraging activities, and environmental enrichment. Rotate toys regularly to maintain novelty and prevent boredom.

5. **Regular Veterinary Care:**

- Schedule regular check-ups with an avian veterinarian to monitor the health and well-being of your Budgerigar and address any potential health issues or concerns promptly. Keep up to date with vaccinations, parasite control, and preventive care measures.

6. **Safe Out-of-Cage Time:**

- Allow Budgerigars supervised out-of-cage time in a safe and secure environment to explore, exercise, and engage in natural behaviors. Ensure that the area is free from hazards and provide opportunities for socialization and mental stimulation.

7. **Environmental Safety:**

- Minimize exposure to potential hazards such as toxic fumes, household chemicals, and predatory pets. Keep the Budgerigar's environment clean, well-ventilated, and free from drafts to promote their health and well-being.

8. **Stress Reduction:**

   - Minimize stressors in the Budgerigar's environment, such as loud noises, sudden movements, and changes in routine, to promote a sense of security and stability. Provide a quiet and predictable environment that allows Budgerigars to feel safe and relaxed.

9. **Monitoring Behavior and Health:**

   - Monitor your Budgerigar's behavior, appetite, and activity levels closely for any signs of illness, injury, or distress. Seek veterinary care promptly if you notice any changes or abnormalities in their behavior or physical condition.

Palliative Care and Euthanasia

As Budgerigars age or face serious health issues, it's essential for caregivers to consider palliative care and, in some cases, euthanasia to ensure their beloved pets are comfortable and free from suffering. Here's a guide on navigating these difficult decisions:

Palliative Care:

1. **Comfort Measures:** Provide a comfortable and stress-free environment for your Budgerigar, ensuring they have access to their favorite perches, toys, and familiar surroundings.

2. **Pain Management:** Work closely with an avian veterinarian to manage any pain or discomfort your Budgerigar may be experiencing. This may involve medication or alternative therapies to alleviate symptoms.

3. **Nutrition and Hydration:** Offer soft foods and fresh water to ensure your Budgerigar receives adequate nutrition and hydration. Consider hand-feeding if they are unable to eat on their own.

4. **Monitoring:** Monitor your Budgerigar's condition closely, observing for changes in behavior, appetite, and activity levels. Keep a record of any symptoms or concerns to discuss with your veterinarian.

5. **Quality of Life Assessment:** Continuously assess your Budgerigar's quality of life, considering factors

such as pain, mobility, and enjoyment of daily activities. Make decisions based on what is in their best interest, prioritizing their comfort and well-being.

Euthanasia:

1. **Consultation:** Discuss euthanasia as a potential option with your avian veterinarian if your Budgerigar's condition worsens and their quality of life becomes significantly compromised.

2. **Consideration:** Consider factors such as pain, suffering, and prognosis when making the decision to euthanize your Budgerigar. It's a difficult decision, but one made out of love and compassion for your pet.

3. **Procedure:** If euthanasia is chosen, your veterinarian will explain the procedure and answer any questions or concerns you may have. The process is typically quick and painless, allowing your Budgerigar to peacefully pass away.

4. **Aftercare:** Discuss aftercare options with your veterinarian, including cremation or burial. Take the time to grieve and remember the special bond you shared with your Budgerigar.

10 | BUDGERIGAR ETIQUETTE AND LEGAL CONSIDERATIONS

Responsible Ownership Practices

Responsible ownership practices are essential for the well-being of Budgerigars and for fostering positive relationships between owners and their pets. Here are some key practices to consider:

1. **Education and Research:** Before acquiring a Budgerigar, educate yourself about their care requirements, behavior, and needs. Research reputable sources, books, and online resources to ensure you understand the responsibilities of Budgerigar ownership.

2. **Choosing the Right Budgerigar:** Select a Budgerigar from a reputable breeder or adoption center, ensuring that the bird is healthy, well-socialized, and suitable for your lifestyle and living situation.

3. **Providing Proper Housing:** Set up a spacious and enriched environment for your Budgerigar, including

a suitable cage or aviary with perches, toys, and nesting materials. Ensure the cage is placed in a safe and secure location away from drafts, direct sunlight, and potential hazards.

4. **Nutritious Diet:** Offer a balanced diet consisting of high-quality seeds, pellets, fresh fruits, and vegetables to meet the nutritional needs of your Budgerigar. Provide fresh water daily and avoid feeding foods that are toxic or harmful to birds.

5. **Regular Veterinary Care:** Schedule regular check-ups with an avian veterinarian to monitor your Budgerigar's health, address any medical concerns, and ensure they receive appropriate vaccinations and preventive care.

6. **Socialization and Enrichment:** Spend time interacting with your Budgerigar daily, providing opportunities for socialization, mental stimulation, and physical exercise. Offer a variety of toys, perches, and activities to keep your Budgerigar engaged and entertained.

7. **Environmental Safety:** Ensure your home is safe and bird-proofed to prevent accidents, injuries, and exposure to toxic substances. Keep doors and

windows closed when your Budgerigar is out of its cage, and supervise interactions with other pets.

8. **Responsible Breeding Practices:** If you decide to breed Budgerigars, do so responsibly, prioritizing the health and welfare of the breeding pair and their offspring. Avoid overbreeding, inbreeding, and breeding birds with known genetic defects or health issues.

9. **Adherence to Legal Requirements:** Familiarize yourself with local laws, regulations, and ordinances pertaining to Budgerigar ownership, breeding, and care. Ensure compliance with licensing, permits, and other legal requirements to avoid fines or penalties.

10. **Lifetime Commitment:** Budgerigars can live for 5 to 10 years or longer with proper care, so be prepared for a long-term commitment to your pet. Ensure you have the time, resources, and dedication to provide for their needs throughout their lifespan.

Legal Requirements and Regulations

When keeping Budgerigars as pets, it's essential to be aware of and comply with any legal requirements and regulations governing their ownership. Here are some common legal considerations:

1. **Licensing and Permitting:** In some areas, owning Budgerigars may require a license or permit from local authorities. Check with your city or municipality to determine if any licensing or permitting requirements apply to Budgerigar ownership in your area.

2. **Import and Export Regulations:** If acquiring Budgerigars from another country or selling them internationally, be aware of any import and export regulations governing the transport and sale of birds. Ensure compliance with customs requirements and obtain any necessary permits or documentation.

3. **Wildlife Protection Laws:** Budgerigars are protected under wildlife protection laws in some regions, particularly in their native habitat of Australia. These laws may restrict the capture, sale, or possession of wild-caught Budgerigars and may require permits for their legal ownership.

4. **Animal Welfare Legislation:** Many jurisdictions have animal welfare legislation in place to protect the well-being of pets, including Budgerigars. These laws

may address issues such as proper housing, nutrition, veterinary care, and prevention of cruelty to animals.

5. **Zoning Regulations:** Check local zoning regulations to ensure compliance with any restrictions on keeping birds, including Budgerigars, in residential areas. Some municipalities may have specific ordinances regarding the types and number of pets allowed in residential properties.

6. **Health and Quarantine Requirements:** When acquiring Budgerigars from breeders or sellers, ensure compliance with any health and quarantine requirements to prevent the spread of infectious diseases. Some regions may have regulations governing the importation of birds and may require health certificates or veterinary inspections.

7. **Breeding Regulations:** If breeding Budgerigars, be aware of any regulations governing breeding practices, including licensing requirements, genetic testing, and registration of breeding facilities. Responsible breeding practices are essential for maintaining the health and welfare of the birds and ensuring compliance with legal requirements.

8. **Sale and Trade Regulations:** When selling or trading Budgerigars, adhere to any regulations governing the sale of pets, including licensing requirements for pet stores or breeders, and consumer protection laws regarding the sale of healthy and properly cared-for animals.

9. **Permitting for Public Exhibitions:** If exhibiting Budgerigars at public events or shows, obtain any necessary permits or approvals from event organizers or regulatory authorities to ensure compliance with local regulations and ensure the welfare of the birds.

10. **Legal Consequences of Non-Compliance:** Failure to comply with legal requirements and regulations governing Budgerigar ownership can result in fines, penalties, confiscation of birds, and legal consequences. It's essential to stay informed and adhere to all applicable laws and regulations to avoid legal issues and ensure the well-being of your Budgerigars.

Interactions with Other Pets

When introducing Budgerigars into a household with other pets, such as dogs or cats, it's crucial to manage interactions carefully to ensure the safety and well-being of all animals involved. Here are some guidelines for introducing Budgerigars to other pets:

1. **Supervised Introductions:** Always supervise interactions between Budgerigars and other pets, especially during the initial introduction phase. Keep the Budgerigar in its cage or aviary and allow other pets to observe from a safe distance.

2. **Gradual Acclimation:** Allow pets to become accustomed to each other's presence gradually. Start by allowing them to see and smell each other from a distance before allowing closer interactions.

3. **Positive Reinforcement:** Use positive reinforcement techniques to encourage calm and respectful behavior from all pets. Reward desirable behaviors such as calmness, curiosity, and gentle interactions with treats, praise, and affection.

4. **Safe Spaces:** Provide separate, secure spaces for each pet to retreat to when they need a break or want to be alone. This can include separate rooms, crates, or designated areas where pets can feel safe and comfortable.

5. **Training and Socialization:** Invest time in training and socializing both your Budgerigar and other pets to ensure they understand appropriate behaviors and boundaries. Teach dogs and cats to respond to commands such as "leave it" or "stay" to prevent unwanted interactions with the Budgerigar.

6. **Precautions for Predatory Pets:** Exercise caution when introducing Budgerigars to pets with a natural prey drive, such as cats or birds of prey. Ensure these pets are closely supervised and never left alone with the Budgerigar unsupervised.

7. **Physical Barriers:** Use physical barriers such as baby gates or pet enclosures to separate pets when necessary, particularly during times when close supervision is not possible, such as when you're away from home or sleeping.

8. **Respect Individual Preferences:** Recognize that not all pets will get along, and some may prefer to keep their distance from each other. Respect each pet's preferences and boundaries to prevent stress or conflict.

9. **Regular Monitoring:** Continuously monitor interactions between pets and be vigilant for any signs

of stress, aggression, or discomfort. Remove the Budgerigar from the situation if it appears anxious or threatened by other pets.

10. **Professional Guidance:** Seek guidance from a professional animal behaviorist or trainer if you encounter difficulties or concerns with pet interactions. They can provide personalized advice and strategies to help facilitate positive relationships between your Budgerigar and other pets.

CONCLUSION

In the journey of caring for Budgerigars as pets, we have explored every aspect of their well-being, from their history and origins to their dietary needs, health care, and interactions with other pets. Throughout this book, we've delved into the intricacies of Budgerigar ownership, offering guidance, insights, and practical tips to help you provide the best possible care for your feathered companions.

As Budgerigar owners, we have the privilege and responsibility of nurturing these intelligent, social, and captivating birds. Through our commitment to responsible ownership practices, we can ensure that Budgerigars thrive in our care, living happy, healthy, and fulfilling lives.

From selecting a Budgerigar and creating the perfect environment to understanding their nutritional needs and providing enrichment and stimulation, we've covered every aspect of Budgerigar care with attention to detail and compassion. We've discussed the importance of regular veterinary care, the signs of a healthy Budgerigar, and how to recognize and address common health issues.

We've also explored the joys and challenges of Budgerigar ownership, from bonding with your Budgerigar and understanding their communication to training and socialization techniques and dealing with behavioral problems. By fostering strong bonds and mutual trust, we can create meaningful connections with our Budgerigars and enrich both their lives and our own.

As we conclude this journey, let us remember that Budgerigars are not just pets—they are cherished companions who bring joy, laughter, and companionship into our lives. By embracing the responsibilities of ownership and honoring the unique needs of our Budgerigars, we can cultivate lifelong relationships built on love, respect, and mutual understanding.

May this book serve as a valuable resource and companion on your journey as a Budgerigar owner, providing guidance, support, and inspiration as you embark on this rewarding and fulfilling adventure. Together, let us celebrate the wonder and beauty of Budgerigars and strive to create a world where every Budgerigar is loved, cherished, and cared for to the fullest extent of our abilities.

Thank you for joining us on this journey, and may your bond with your Budgerigar continue to flourish and thrive for years to come.

Printed in Great Britain
by Amazon